Formatting eBooks with Open Office Writer

Formatting eBooks
with
Open Office Writer

Dr. Kerry R. Bunn

Author: Dr. Kerry R. Bunn, Sr.
krbunn.com ❖ krbunn.blogspot.com
Published September 2010   CS
10 9 8 7 6 5 4 3 2 1

September 23, 2010 -- 9:00 AM
v1.1 -- October 1 -- 6:00 AM

ISBN: 1453764259

EAN-13: 9781453764251

Paperback Available

Open Office Writer is part of the OpenOffice.Org project.

Formatting eBooks with Open Office Writer

Dr. Kerry R. Bunn

Contents

~ ~ ~

1. Getting Started

My guess is you have struggled like I have in correctly formatting your eBook for publication. I was frustrated and tired of experimenting to see what worked and what did not work. I finally decided to develop a guide to simplify creating and formatting eBooks.

This guide is designed for formatting eBooks using Open Office Writer version 3.0 and greater. The basic principles in this guide should work equally well with any word processor. These step-by-step instructions are easy to follow and help authors correctly format their documents in eBook format.

I am working under the assumption that each person reading this book has some basic knowledge about using their computer and Open Office Writer. While this is not a primer on word processing, I have included step-by-step illustrations in this book for those who may not be fully familiar with all features of Open Office Writer. It would be a good idea to use the "help" feature of Open Office Writer to become familiar with some of its basic operations. Help and support for Open Office Writer can be found at http://support.openoffice.org. The Open Office Writer's Guide 3 (a collaborative work of several authors) can also be downloaded for free from my website at http://krbunn.com/ebook.html.

As you work through this guide, you will create (1) a clean eBook page style, (2) various eBook paragraph styles, and (3) an eDocument template for easy access to creating new eBooks. You will develop the skills to properly apply styles and formatting with consistency to maximize readability on a variety of eReaders. You will also be exposed to the basic elements of Table of Contents, hyperlinks, and working with graphics.

New technology, hardware, software, firmware, and future eReader developments ultimately means that what I have written here will be out-of date. But for the time being, it works with the technology currently available.

I included links to my complete eDocument Template (free) at the end of this guide. This should speed up the preliminary work of creating your eBook masterpiece and is my way of saying "thanks" for buying and reading this guide.

Disclaimer: This formatting guide works well for me. But since every author, typist, and eBook are unique, and I am not doing your actual physical formatting, I can make no absolute guarantee that your document will format correctly. But I think it will!

One more important note. It is always best to create, edit and save your file in the particular format required by your ePublisher. If your ePublisher needs an HTML file, then edit and save your document as HTML. If they require Word.DOC, then edit and save as a Word.DOC.

~ ~ ~

2. eBook and Paperback

I published this guide in both eBook and paperback formats. The paperback edition purposely looks as close as possible to the eBook edition. I let the text and graphics flow from page to page as they would in an eReader.

I checked my eBook on a Nook® Reader, software version 1.41. The Cambria 12 point font is somewhat similar to the Nook Light Classic, Large font. Though not an exact match, it displays this text well in my Nook®. I used the same basic document file to create both eBook and paperback formats with a few exceptions.

(1) The eBook edition does not display "headers" or "footers."

(2) Since the eBook edition is not bound by "pages," I did not use page-breaks in the paperback edition except to start new sections/chapters at the next page top. I like my eBooks to start new sections/chapters at the top of a new screen. The paperback also starts each main section/chapter at the top of a clean page.

(3) The amount of material on each page will vary between the eBook and paperback. You will see various amounts of "white space" after "~ ~ ~" in this paperback and eBooks. This simulates the various page flows and white space caused by different eBooks font sizes.

(4) I used single spacing in the eBook. I used Registry-true: Active and Proportional spacing of 125% in the paperback.

(5) The eBook uses hyperlinks and bookmarks, not page numbers in the Table of Contents. The paperback uses page numbers.

(6) Graphics are saved as 167 DPI GIF files and do not exceed 501 pixels in width. Because the graphics were screen captures at 96 DPI and then re-sized, the eBooks graphics may be difficult to read for some individuals in an eReader. This will happen with your work and graphics too.

(7) Graphics in the eBook and paperback may not always appear on the same screen/page with the preceding paragraph.

(8) The Front Matter and Copyright pages differ in eBooks and paperbacks.

~ ~ ~

3. Important eTerms

Here are some important eTerms you need to be familiar with. I use these terms throughout this book.

eBook: a collection of text or images in digital format designed to be read on devices such as Amazon's Kindle®, Barnes & Noble's Nook®, Sony's eReader®, Boarder's Kobo eReader®, etc.

eCreator/eConvertor: software programs such as Smashwords© "Meatgrinder" that converts eDocuments into eBook file formats. Mobipocket Creator® and Calibri eBook Management© are also examples of eCreators and can be downloaded from the Internet.

eDocument: your document that will be converted to an eBook.

eFont: the text characters displayed on an eReader screen.

eInk: the term used to describe the look of text on an eReader display.

ePublishing: the process of converting an eDocument into an eBook.

eReader: the physical devices designed to read eBooks.

eUser: the person who reads the eBook.

I use   "~ ~ ~"   to mark each section/chapter break in

both the eBook and paperback editions.

~ ~ ~

4. A Word about eReaders

Formatting eDocuments for eReaders is different than formatting a document for paperback publication. Here are some important issues to consider when preparing your eDocument for publication.

eReaders use varieties of HTML-like formatting commands for displaying eDocuments. This brings us to the first hurdle to overcome in creating your eBook. As an author, you are not writing HTML code, you are writing an eDocument. Your goal therefore, is to create an eDocument that will successfully convert to an eReader HTML-like format. To further complicate matters, each eReader supplier has their own special tweaks for their device's "native" format.

Your finished document will be converted to an eReader format during the publication process. Different eCreators may convert the same eBook and produce slight variances. Your finished eBook will look slightly different on each brand of eReader. The final format of your eBook is eReader device dependent. This is just a fact of life in the ePublishing world.

eReaders have limited font styles, face, and size. Most people do not have access to these proprietary eReader fonts. You will not be able to match your Open Office Writer (or any word processor) fonts to your eReader.

Keep your font selection simple. Fonts like Arial, Garamond, or New Times Roman seem to convert easiest.

Traditional point sizes (such as 11, 12, 13, etc.) do not apply to eReaders. eFonts are arranged according to size groups. Size One is approximately 8 points and smaller. Size Two includes 9, 10, and 11 point fonts. Size Three includes 12 and 13 point fonts. Size Four covers 14, 15, and 16 points. Size Five includes 17 and 18 points and size Six is over 18 points. Each eReader manufacture sets their own point values and those values will vary between eReader brands.

eReaders have limited screen resolution. A common screen resolution size is 600 x 800 pixels, 167 DPI (dots per inch. This is different than your computer screen. You cannot match your computer screen resolution to an eReader. Do not spend the time and effort trying to create a page size and font combination to match an eReader screen. One simple size change by an eUser to their settings will negate all your "matching" efforts. For example, have you ever changed your computer monitor resolution? Did your desktop icons move?

eReaders pay little attention to pages and margins. This is because eDocuments are dynamic not static. eReader devices and eUsers generally decide their own display settings according to device limitations. Ideally, eDocuments should flow smoothly on every eReader for every eUser's personal preference. It is a good idea to make your eBook as readable on as many devices as possible.

~ ~ ~

5. Working with Page Styles

5.1 Creating a Clean eDocument

While eBooks do not have "pages" as such, Open Office Writer does. So, we will work with pages first. Let's start with a new, clean eDocument to define our eBook formatting. By creating, saving, and using a clean eBook page style you avoid hidden formatting marks in your document. Hidden formatting can cause lots of weeping and gnashing of teeth when working with eBooks.

Once you have worked through this guide, you will have created a complete eBook document template. At that point, you can simply open the eBook document template and begin your typing. But for now, go ahead and create a clean page style.

Start Open Office Writer. If you run Open Office Writer from the Open Office Suite option, start Open Office Suite and select the **Text <u>D</u>ocument** option in the center box (see figure 01).

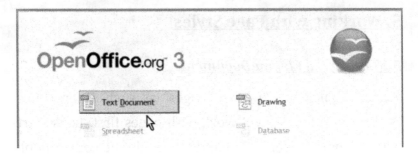

figure 01

Open Office Writer should be open on your screen.

If you bypass Open Office Suite and run Open Office Writer direct, start Open Office Writer and open a new document by selecting **File**, **New**, **Text Document** (see figure 02).

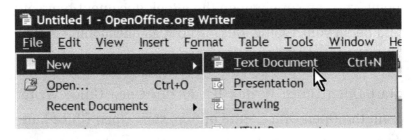

figure 02

5.2 Creating a Page Style

Now, we will create a "Page Style" to be used for your eBooks. Using Open Office Writer's Styles and Formatting feature is a good way to ensure consistency and correct formatting to all parts of your eBook.

Using the mouse, access Styles and Formatting by selecting **Format**, **Styles and Formatting F11** from the Open Office Menu Bar (see figure 03).

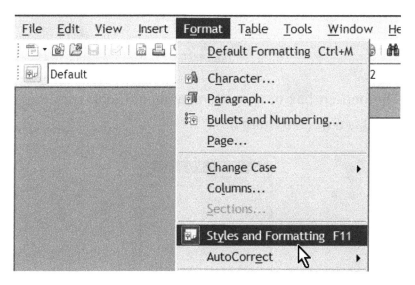

figure 03

When you click on **Styles and Formatting F11**, you should see the Styles and Formatting pop-up box on your screen. Click on the fourth icon from the left at the top of the pop-up box (see figure 04). This is the "Page Styles" section .

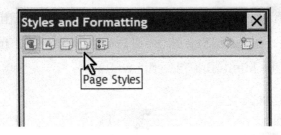

figure 04

The pop-up box on your screen should look something like this now (see figure 05).

figure 05

Click on **ALL** in the drop down arrow at the right, bottom of the pop-up box (see figure 06).

figure 06

Click on **Custom Styles**. Your Styles and Formatting pop-up box should look something like this (see figure 07).

figure 07

We will now create a custom page style for eBooks. Place your cursor inside of the pop-up box and **right click** the Mouse. The word **[New ...]** will appear (see figure 8). Click it.

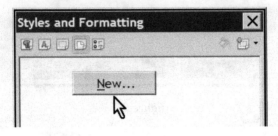

figure 08

The Page Style pop-up box will appear and be on the **[Organizer]** tab (see figure 9).

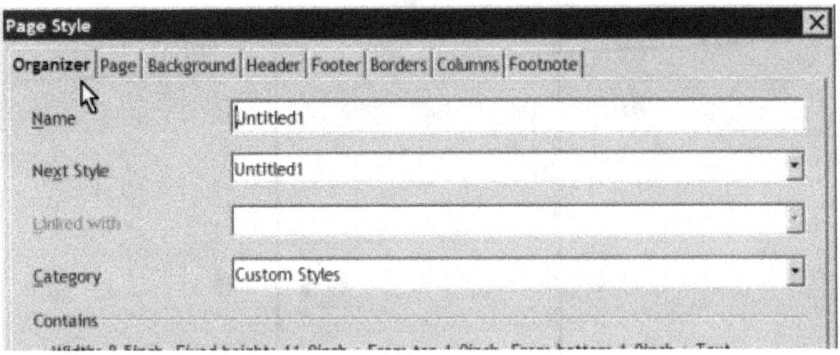

figure 9

I name my page styles for clarity even though eBooks generally use only one page style. This is helpful for locating your eBook style if the Styles and Formatting box is ever set to "All Styles."

I will name my style "eBook Page Default." To rename your page style, click on **Untitled1** in the name box and type in your new name. My newly titled eBook page style looks like this (see figure 10). Notice that the **Next Style** box updated to the new name automatically.

Do **NOT** click **[OK]** yet.

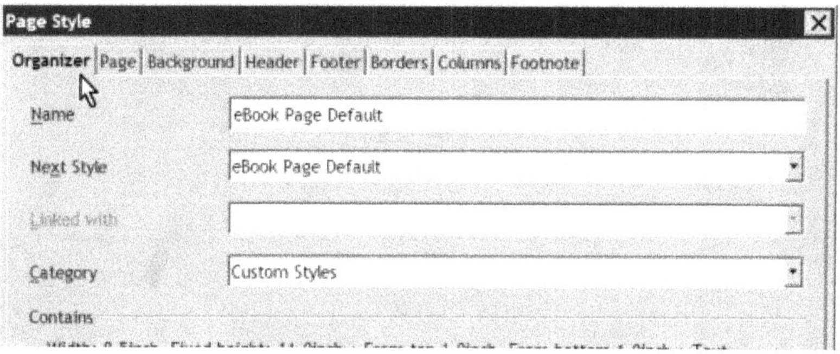

figure 10

5.3 Setting Up Page Formatting

Click on the **[Page]** tab. Your screen should look something like this (see figure 11).

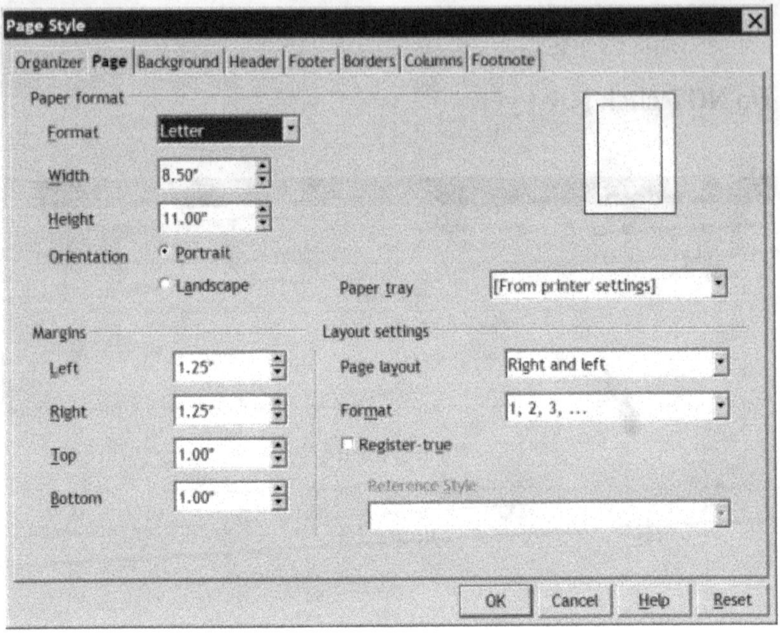

figure 11

Now let's define the page format. I know what you are thinking. Yes, I said "eBooks pay little attention to pages or margins." So, why worry with setting them? Because someone, somewhere may want to print a hard copy of your document; especially if they download your document in PDF format. It would be good if your document looked nice when printed.

If you desire to use a standard "letter-like" format, which is the default page format for Open Office Writer, just click on **[OK]** and your "eBook Page Default" is now set.

Since this particular document is offered in eBook and

paperback format, I will use my paperback book settings for instructional purposes. Adapt your settings as desired. If you use my eBook/Paperback style, your screen should look like this when everything is set (see figure 12).

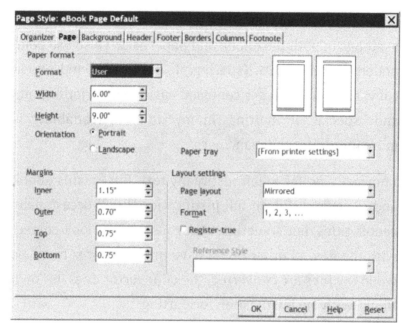

figure 12

Your "eBook Page Default" style is now set for creating your eBooks. Click on **[OK]** to save your work.

Now, every time you begin a new eBook, simply select and apply the "eBook Page Default" style and you are ready to begin typing your eDocument.

~ ~ ~

6. <u>Working for Screen Readability</u>

I like things kept simple. Less is more! Basically, use one simple font with a few sizes and effects. Remember, you cannot exactly match an eReader font anyway.

I used Cambria 12 point type for text and 14 point type for headings in both the eBook and paperback. I also use bold, underline, and italics (sparingly). HTML files and eBook converters seem to get confused easily with a lot of fonts and "special" formatting. In my opinion, readability is more important than fanciness.

I normally prefer to left justify my text. But for this eBook and paperback I used full justification. I will occasionally center titles, but sometimes they just do not look correct with the flow of other text. I have noticed that sometimes when my files are converted, the eConvertor does its "own thing" with my justification formatting.

Here is an important concept to remember. Printed books are static. You format them to look good to the eye and they do not change. eBooks are dynamic and change according to the eReader and personal preference. Format eBooks primarily for readability.

Once you have mastered the techniques used in this eBook, your eBooks should read well on an eReader.

~ ~ ~

7. Working with Paragraphs

7.1 Creating Paragraph Styles

Here is an important concept to remember. Everything that is not a single character in a line of text should be considered a paragraph. Technically, even a single character by itself is a paragraph too. You work with paragraphs in eBooks, not individual lines or characters. Develop the habit of thinking of your material in paragraphs not as individual lines or characters.

It is helpful to plan which styles and formats you will need in your eDocument. This way, when you create each style you can set all the necessary formatting as you create that style.

By creating and applying paragraph styles, you can make global changes to your paragraphs throughout your eBook. Change the default paragraph style and you change your entire eBook. This can be a good thing!

Avoid making changes directly to an individual paragraph. This is not a good thing! Remember the goal is to ensure consistency and correct formatting to all parts of your eBook.

By applying paragraph styles to everything, your eBook will meet that goal. But use common sense about this, you really do not need dozens of paragraph styles.

When you have finished creating your custom paragraph styles, you will have set the proper font, size, line spacing, extra spacing, indention, justification, etc. for each particular paragraph style. You will then apply your paragraph styles to sections of text.

7.2 Setting a "Default" Master Document Font

Some eConvertors will utilize a documents "default" or "normal" font settings as the standard font for the finished eBook. This does not mean the eConvertor will use and print your font--it will not. It does mean that if the main font used in your eDocument text is **not** the same as the "normal" font, most eConvertors will create a lot of extra coding to handle font changes. To avoid extra overhead, we need to set a "default" Master Document Font.

Select **Tools**, **Options** from the Open Office Writer Main Menu Bar. Click (or double-click) on the **OpenOffice.org Writer** option and then select **Basic Fonts (Western)**. Set all font options to match the main font of your eDocument (see figure 13). I have used Cambria as my font. Click **[OK]** to save your work when you have finished.

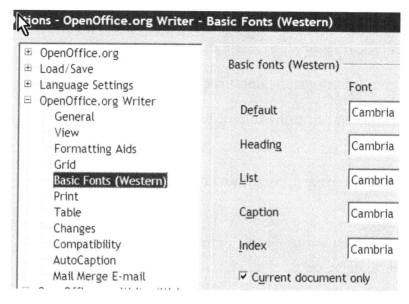

figure 13

7.3 My Basic Paragraph Styles

Here are some basic paragraph styles. You may or may not need all of these styles for your eDocument. Adapt as needed for your particular application. Since each of these styles is linked to the "eBook Paragraph--Default" style, you only need to change certain parameters to define a new style.

eBook Paragraph--Default: Cambria, 12 point, regular, left-alignment. This should be identical to the "Default" font style and your Master Document Font. It has no additional line spacing. This style should be kept as simple as possible.

eBook Paragraph--Block Justified: 0.12 inch spacing after paragraph.

eBook Paragraph--Centered: centered

eBook Paragraph--Indent Justified: 0.33 inch indent, justified.

eBook Paragraph--Single Lines: 0.12 inch spacing after paragraph.

eBook Heading--Main: 14 point font, bold, 0.14 inch spacing below paragraph, Outline level: Level 1.

eBook Heading--Sub: 14 point font, italic, 0.24 inch spacing above paragraph, 0.12 inch spacing below paragraph, Outline level: Level 2.

eBook Heading--Underline: underline, 0.12 inch spacing below paragraph, Outline level: Level 3.

Notes: "Registry-true: Active" and "Proportional Spacing" of 125% are used for my paperback books. eConvertors seem to ignore these settings for now. If you decide to use Proportional Spacing, check your published file carefully. Spacing above and spacing after are based on the current font; i.e. 12 point font equals approximately 0.12 inches before or after spacing.

OK, let's create an eBook paragraph style. I will show you how to create my "eBook Paragraph--Default" and my "eBook Text--Indent Justify" styles. You can follow these instructions and create additional styles as needed.

7.4 Creating the "eBook Paragraph--Default" Style

By now you should be a little more familiar working with Styles and Formatting. You will be working with Styles and Formatting a lot when creating eBooks. You may want to review the Open Office Help about Styles and Formatting. We will now create the "eBooks Paragraph--Default" style.

Advanced users will notice that this style is not really necessary since it is identical to the "default" paragraph style. But since I prefer to locate my styles quickly and easily, I created this style and stored it under "Custom Styles" for quick reference.

Access Styles and Formatting by selecting **Format**, **Styles and Formatting F11** from the Open Office Menu Bar. This is similar to what you have already done in creating a page style. Click on the first icon at the left at the top of the pop-up box (see figure 14). This is the "Paragraph Styles" section.

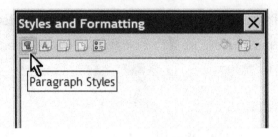

figure 14

If you are not displaying "Custom Styles" at the bottom of the pop-up box, Click the drop-down arrow in the right, bottom corner and select **Custom Styles**. Refer back to figure 07 if you need additional help.

Place your cursor inside of the pop-up box and right-click the mouse. The word **[New ...]** will appear (refer back to figure 10 if you need help). Click it. The Paragraph Style box will be on the **[Organizer]** tab. I named my first style "eBook Paragraph--Default." To rename your paragraph style, select **Untitled1** in the **Name** box and type in the new style name. The **Next Style** box will automatically update to the new name. My newly titled eBook paragraph style looks like this (see figure 15). Do **NOT** click **[OK]**.

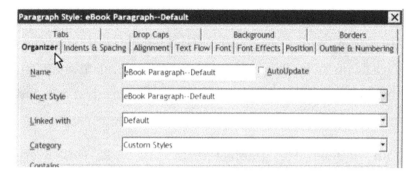

figure 15

This is very important! Be sure the **Linked with** box (see figure 15) is set to "Default" and the **Category** box is set to "Custom Styles."

We will now verify the font and font point size with this newly created style. Click the **[Font]** tab and set your preferences for the "Font, Type Face," and "Size" for your eDocument. (see figure 16). This should be the same font and size set as your "default" font and your Master Document Font.

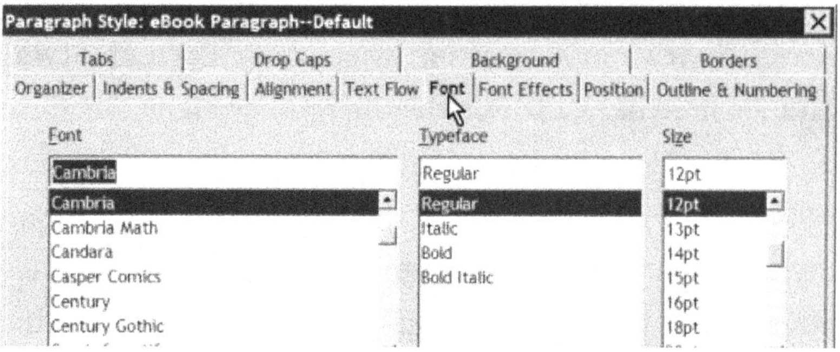

figure 16

You can also set other document-wide formats such as indents, spacings, etc., by making changes to this default paragraph style. Think of this as a "global default style." To change any feature, simply click on the desired tab and make your changes. Click on **[OK]** to save your work.

Your "eBook Paragraph--Default style" is set. Every paragraph in your eBook will eventually be linked to this default paragraph style. Change this style and it will change your entire eBook.

7.5 Creating the "eBook Paragraph--Indent Justify" Style

By now you should be somewhat familiar with using "Styles and Formatting F11." I will not repeat every graphical step from this point forward. Refer back to previous examples if needed.

Follow the same basic steps used for creating the "eBook Paragraph--Default" style to create additional styles. Access Styles and Formatting by selecting **Format**, **Styles and Formatting F11** from the Open Office Menu Bar. Click on the first icon on the left at the top of the pop-up box. This is the "Paragraph Styles" section. Make sure "Custom Styles" is displayed at the bottom of the pop-up box. Place your cursor inside of the pop-up box and right click the mouse. The word **[New ...]** will appear. Click it. The

"Paragraph Style" box will be on the **[Organizer]** tab. To rename your paragraph style, click on **Untitled1** in the **Name** box and type in your new name. I used "eBook Paragraph --Indent Justify."

The **Next Style** will automatically update to the new name. If it does not, click the drop-down arrow for **Next Style** and select "eBook Paragraph--Indent Justify."

Now click the drop-down arrow for **Linked with** and choose "eBook Paragraph--Default." This is an important step and links this paragraph style with the default paragraph style. Make sure **AutoUpdate** is **NOT** checked. Your pop-up box should look something like this now (see figure 17).

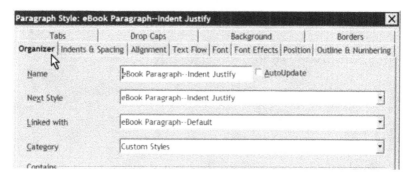

figure 17

All format options for this paragraph style are now associated with and linked to the "eBook Paragraph--Default style." Do **not** click **[OK]** yet!

Since we are linked to the "eBook Paragraph--Default" style, our font and other settings are already preset. For the "eBook Paragraph--Indent Justified" style, we only need to change the indents and set the alignment.

Click the **[Indents & Spacings]** tab. Change the 0.00" in the **First line** box to 0.25" or 0.33" for a standard indent. You can adapt the size as needed. Do not use large sizes, they just do not look good. Also, I have better success specifying a size rather than selecting the "Automatic indent" box.

I have found that line spacing works best when set to single or 1.5 line spacing. "Proportional Spacing" and "Registry-true: Active" should be avoided in eBooks because it may cause your eBook to be rejected by the eConvertor and eDistributors.

Your pop-up box should look like this (see figure 18).

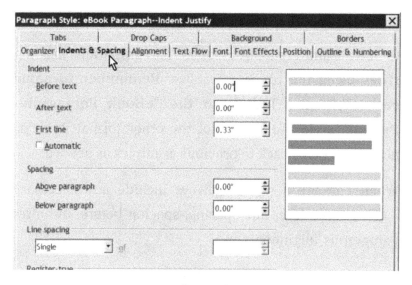

figure 18

Now click on the **[Alignment]** tab and select "Justified" for your text alignment option (see figure 19).

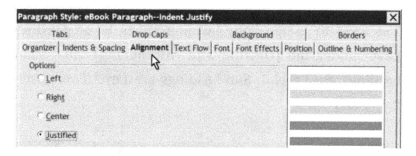

figure 19

You just created the "eBook Paragraph--Indent Justify" style. Click on **[OK]** to save your work.

7.6 Creating Other Paragraph Styles

Go ahead and create your other paragraph and heading styles using the processes above. **Remember to name each style and link it to the "eBook Paragraph--Default" style.** Adjust any of the other format items as necessary. Refer back to previous examples as needed.

When I create a style, I always include any necessary indents, type face, line spacing, spacing before and after paragraphs, alignments, etc.

Since all my styles are linked to the "eBook Paragraph--Default," I only need to change formatting for items specific to each new style.

7.7 Heading Styles

You need to assign your heading styles to an **Outline Level** under the **[Outline and Numbering]** tab. Main headings are Level 1, Sub headings are Level 2, etc. (see figure 20).

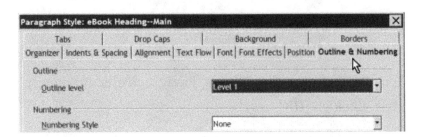

figure 20

7.8 Setting the Hyperlink Font Color

Hyperlinked items in Open Office Writer may or may not appear in different color fonts in your document and may or may not be shaded in your final eDocument. Shaded fonts do do not make for easy readability. It is probably best to set the hyperlink font colors to black.

Select **Tools**, **Options** from the Main Menu Bar. This will bring up the "Options" pop-up box. Double click on OpenOffice.Org to expand the selection list. Click on Appearance. Scroll down to **Unvisited Links** and **Visited Links** under the "User interface elements" column. Set both values to black.

~ ~ ~

8. Saving an eDocument Template

Now that you have created your page and paragraph styles, it would be wise to save them for future use. I have noticed that Open Office Writer does not always remember "Custom Styles" when a new document is created.

There is an easy way to make sure your "Custom Styles" are saved for future use. We will save a blank document as a document template. This will save all formatting associated with your eDocument.

To do so, select **File**, **Templates**, **Save** from the Menu Bar. Type in the name of your new eDocument template and click **[OK]** (see figure 21). I used "eDocument-template-ebook" as my file name.

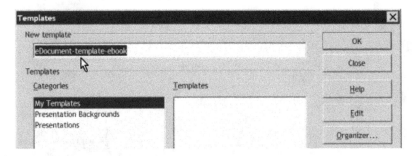

figure 21

The next time you want to create an eBook, simply open this template and begin creating. To open an existing template select **File**, **New**, **Templates and Documents** from the Menu Bar. Click on the **Templates** icon in the left-hand column. Choose the desired template from the "Template and Documents" pop-up box and click **[OK]**. (see figure 22)

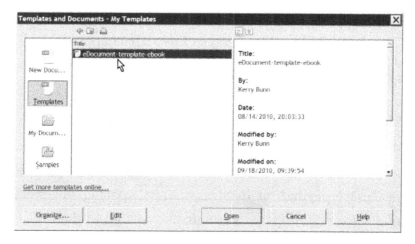

figure 22

8.1 Download eDocument Template

You can download my completed eDocument Template for free from my website at krbunn.com. This is my way of saying "thanks" for reading this guide. You will need to save a copy of my templates to your templates location.

Template #1 (for eBooks only) can be downloaded free of charge from at http://krbunn.com/ebook.html.

The "eDocument-template-ebook.ott" file is for creating eBooks only and does not include any paperback pagination or proportional spacing. This is the best option for non-paperback publishers. Page size is set to 6x9 with 0.50 margins.

8.2 Paperback Template Notes

Template #2 (for eBooks and 6x9 paperbacks) can be downloaded free of charge from my website at http://krbunn.com/ebook

The "eDocument-template-both.ott" file is identical to the one used to create this eBook and paperback. It is formatted to correctly print a 6x9 paperback with all necessary pagination, headers, footers, spacing, etc. Most eConvertors will strip the items not needed in the eBook conversion process. This means you possibly only need one completed document for creating both eBooks and paperbacks.

I included additional page styles in the paperback document template. These styles are necessary for Front Matter, Title Pages, Cover Pages, etc. required for hard-copy books.

~ ~ ~

9. Modifying an Existing Style

To modify an existing style, first select the desired style from the Styles and Formatting pop-up box. Pressing **[F11]** is a good short-cut for opening and closing the Styles and Formatting pop-up box. Right click on the selected style using the mouse. Click on **Modify** (see figure 23). Now you can change the selected style as needed.

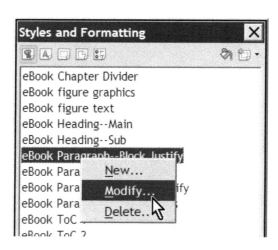

figure 23

There are two buttons on the Paragraph Styles pop-up box that need special attention (see figure 24).

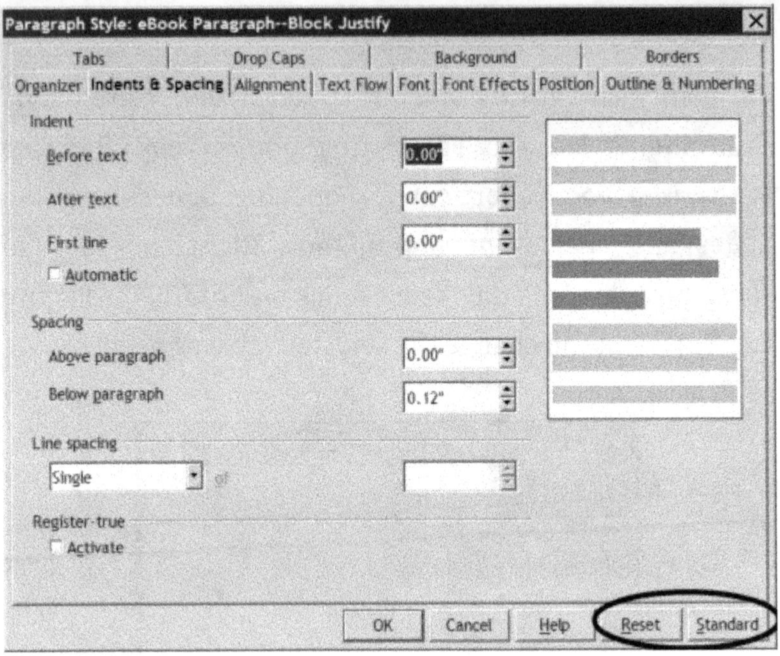

figure 24

The first is the **[Reset]** button. Clicking this button will reset the pop-up box parameters to exactly how it was when you opened the box. This is helpful if you are experimenting with changes. If you do not like how things look, click **[Reset]** and everything will reset.

The **[Standard]** button resets all formatting back to its original state. In our case, everything is set back to "eBook Paragraph--Default." Remember, we linked all styles to this style as our default.

~ ~ ~

10. Adding Blank Lines and Spacing

Blank lines and extra spacing are added to your eBook by modifying paragraph styles. When properly set, you never have to press **[Enter]** to add blank lines to your text except for special formatting situations.

For example, my "eBook Paragraph--Block Justify" style sets 0.12 points below the paragraph. This is necessary because "block text" needs spacing between paragraphs for readability. Since I am using 12 point type, 0.12 points after the paragraph equals one blank line. Adjust this as desired (refer back to figure 24).

~ ~ ~

11. Setting Up the Next Style

You can automate a lot of basic formatting by setting up the "Next Style" for every paragraph and heading style. When you apply formatting to a particular paragraph or heading, the "Next Style" is automatically applied to the following paragraph or heading.

Using and applying formatting automatically saves a lot of time and work for the author. I formatted this entire eBook automatically by using this process. Here is what the formatting looks like applied to the next three paragraphs listed.

My eBook Heading--Main (this style) is followed by my eBook Heading--Sub

My eBook Heading--Sub (this style) is followed by my eBook Paragraph - Indent Justify

My default paragraph style (eBook Paragraph--Block Justify: this style) is now automatically set for regular typing such as you see in this paragraph.

Generally, the next style assigned to my "eBook Heading--Sub" is the main paragraph style for my eDocuments. Your styles may be different depending on your needs and style names.

To setup your next style, choose the style you want to modify and open it for modification. Select the **[Organizer]** tab. In this example, the "eBook Heading-- Sub" is already Linked with "eBook Paragraph--Default." All we need to do now is define the "Next Style" to use. Click on the drop-down arrow in the **Next Style** box. Search for and select the style you want to follow in the next paragraph.

I chose "eBook Paragraph--Block Justify" as my **Next Style**. You would choose your basic paragraph style as next. Your pop-up box should look like this (see figure 25).

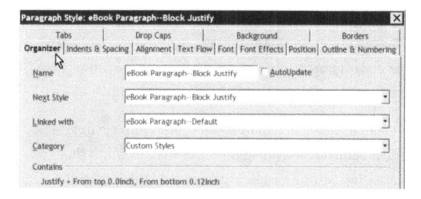

Figure 25

Remember to click **[OK]** to save your work. Also remember to save any changes you make to your eDocument template.

~ ~ ~

12. Typing, Formatting, and Styles

Now, let's spend some time talking about typing the eDocument itself. To successfully format an eBook, you may need to unlearn some basic typing. Pages are liquid in eBooks. They change and flow according to the eReader and the preferences and settings chosen by the person reading the eBook. Chances are very good that your eBook will not look like your typed copy. That is OK, that's what happens.

Do not use text boxes, frames, tables, auto-bullets or auto-numbering, wingdings, or any other special formatting in your eDocument. Tturn off Writer's Auto Correct feature.

 Do not use multiple **[Enter]**s to put blank spaces between your paragraphs when you type. If you have setup your styles correctly, this is handled automatically.

Do not use headers, footers, footnotes, or page numbers. Most eConvertors will ignore these settings, but they can cause formatting issues. If you include them in your eDocument, be sure to check your finished work.

Do not use two spaces after a period or colon.

Do not use the **[TAB]** key ever!

Do not press **[ENTER]** after every line in a paragraph. Let Open Office Writer automatically wrap your line endings.

Only press **[ENTER]** when you are creating a new paragraph or heading.

Do not use the **[SPACE BAR]** to force items to lineup on the screen. This will NOT work in any eBook reader.

~ ~ ~

13. Applying Styles and Formatting

This entire eBook was spaced and formatted using the methods described in this guide. There are no extra **[ENTER]**s anywhere in this document. Everything was accomplished by creating and applying formatting and styles. I applied my first style when I began typing. Since I linked my styles with the "Next Style" most of my formatting was handled automatically.

Applying a "paragraph style" or "header style" to existing text is easy. Simply select the text you want to "style," then select the desired style from the "Styles and Formatting" pop-up box. I generally keep the "Styles and Formatting" pop-up box on my screen (over on the side of the page) for easy accessibility.

Sometimes you may need to select a paragraph or heading and then apply the "Default Formatting" option to correctly apply formatting. Right click the selected paragraph or heading and then select Default Formatting to force the selected item to reformat.

I do not think it is a good idea to tweak the formatting of individual paragraphs, you will eventually forget which paragraph you changed, what changes you made, and why you made them. Instead, create a new paragraph style and apply it to the text. Again, use common sense and avoid creating dozens of paragraph styles.

There will be a few occasions where main and sub headings just do not look spaced correctly. In those cases, I will adjust the spacing manually. To do so, select the header or sub-header to be changed. Right click on the selected item (the actual text, not the style selection) with the mouse. Select **P̲aragraph....** This will open the "Paragraph" pop-up box on your screen. Now you can adjust the spacing of the selected header or sub-header only. This does not change the spacing of your defined styles.

~ ~ ~

14. Adding Page Breaks

There are occasions when you will want to force a page break in your text. With some eReaders/eCreators (not all though), a forced line break will cause the next paragraph to appear at the top of the eReader screen. This gives the illusion of going to the top of the next page.

Adding a line break is easy. Place your cursor where you want the line beak to begin. Press **[Ctrl]+[Enter]**. That's it. If you add line breaks to existing text, you may need to reapply your style to the paragraph following the break.

14.1Automatic Page Breaks

Some eReaders and eConvertors will automatically start at the top of a new screen with every "Level 1" heading. Some eReaders and eConvertors automatically start every section labeled with "Chapter" at the top of a new screen also.

Be sure to check your completed eBooks to verify that "page breaks" occur in their proper place. This is life in the wonderful (but not standardized yet) world of eBook formatting!

~ ~ ~

15. Checking for Hidden Text

Hidden text can cause all types of problems in correctly formatting your book for an eReader. To check for hidden text of characters select **<u>V</u>iew**, **<u>N</u>onprinting Characters** from the Open Office Menu Bar. When you click on **<u>N</u>onprinting Characters** you will see additional characters on your screen. Open Office Help defines what the formatting marks are. Repeat this process to turn-off the view feature.

You can also use "View" to see text boundaries, field names, shading and hidden paragraphs. With View turned on, you can remove any unnecessary character, spacing, etc. to make sure your eDocument is correctly formatted. Remember, you do not want to use **[Tab]** anywhere in your document.

Since every style I use is linked to my "eBook Paragraph--Default," I can make global changes to my entire document. I will often change the main font to something like "wingdings" (in my eBook Paragraph--Default style). Then every paragraph or heading with an applied "style" will have the new font (wingding) and I can easily spot the sections that have not been "styled." After making any necessary changes, I reset my main font in the "eBook Paragraph--Default style."

~ ~ ~

16. Creating a Table of Contents

16.1 Table of Contents by Chapter Headings

The first option for creating a Table of Contents is by using "key words" or "markers" in your eDocument. Some eConvertors will automatically mark any line beginning with the word "Chapter" as a Table of Contents item. Other eConvertors may allow for special markers such at <TOC> or <h1> to denote Table of Contents items. You would need to check your eConvertor requirements for conformity.

16.2 Table of Contents by Bookmarks and Hyperlinks

The other option for creating a Table of Contents is through the use of Bookmarks and Hyperlinks. Mark Coker's The Smashwords Style Guide© (see Smashwords.com) has a good section on creating a Table of Contents through this method. He credits Smashwords author, Cheryl Anne Gardner, for sharing her Table of Contents tips which Coker augmented. I want to acknowledge both of those authors and then add my own thoughts on creating a Table of Contents.

From my own trial and error experience, it is best to create the Table of Contents last. Moving, changing, or renaming a "content" item can cause your contents bookmarks and hyperlinks to fail. It takes a lot a repetitive work to create a functioning Table of Contents. Be patient, take your time, check your links and everything will eventually work.

First, type your Table of Contents material as plain text at the desired location in your eDocument. Be sure to give your Table of Contents a name. Do not auto-generate your Table of Contents. It will not work in eReaders.

Second, move your cursor to the very beginning of your Table of Contents title. I used "Contents" as my title. Now select **Insert**, **Bookmark** from the Main Menu Bar. Type "contents" in the name box as the name for this bookmark and click **[OK]**. Do not create bookmarks for the line items in your Table of Contents.

Third, move your cursor to the very beginning of the first heading in your text (not in the Table of Contents). Create a bookmark for this heading selecting **Insert**, **Bookmark** from the Main Menu Bar. Type a name you can easily remember in the name box as the name for this bookmark and click **[OK]**. Bookmarks cannot have spaces in their names. Repeat this procedure for each header in your text you want to link to the Table of Contents.

Fourth, now we will create hyperlinks to the newly created bookmarks. Go back to the very first line item entry (not title) in your Table of Contents and select it.

Fifth, select **Insert**, **Hyperlink** from the Main Menu Bar. The Hyperlink pop-up box will appear. Click on the **Document** icon option in the left-hand column. Your pop-up box should now look like this (see figure 26).

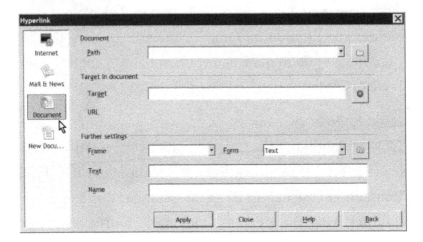

figure 26

Now click on the **"bulls-eye"** in the **Target in document** section of the pop-up box (see figure 27).

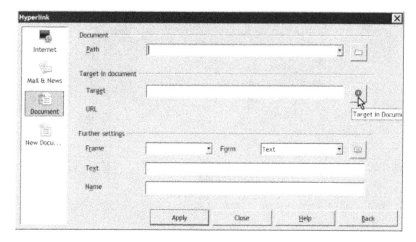

figure 27

A second pop-up box will not open. It is the "Target in Document" box. Double-click **Bookmarks** in the pop-up box to expand the headings list (see figure 28).

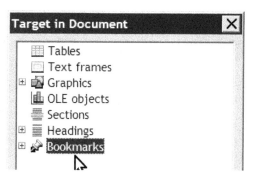

figure 28

Double-click on appropriate bookmark that your Table of Contents item should point to (see figure 29). I selected "Contents" as an example, you would select your headings.

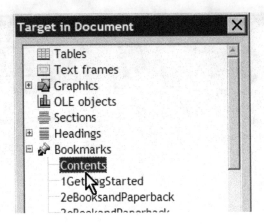

figure 29

Your selection will now be listed as the **Target** in the "Target in Document" section of the Hyperlink pop-up box (see figure 30). Click on **[Apply]** and then **[Close]** on the Hyperlink pop-up box to save your hyperlink.

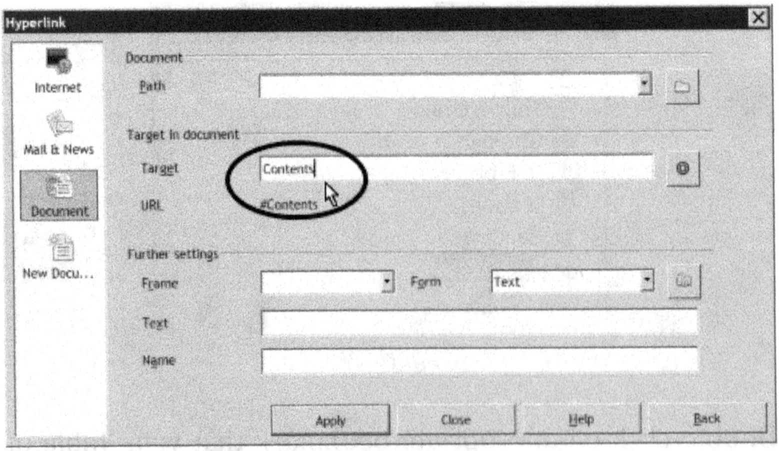

figure 30

Six, repeat steps four and five for each line item in your Table of Contents. Be sure to select the heading that matched your Table of Contents entry.

Seven, now continue to your headings in the eDocument text and repeat steps four and five for each individual heading making sure to link every heading back to the title for your Table of Contents. In my eDocument, the title is named "Contents." Every heading is linked back to the title of the Table of Contents.

Finally, make sure that all of your hyperlinks work. You can do this by pressing and holding the **[Ctrl]** and clicking on a heading or Table of Contents item. When properly configured, each link will take you to the correct location.

Confused Yet? Breath deep, relax, and try again!

~ ~ ~

17. Converting Existing Documents

If you are converting an existing document to an eBook and are having severe problems with the formatting, I suggest doing the following. It is an extreme option and will remove all formatting from your document. Always have a backup copy of your document before removing existing formatting.

Open you document in Open Office Writer. Select the entire document by pressing **[Ctrl] A**. Then press **[Ctrl] M** to remove all formatting. I do mean this will remove ALL formatting. You now have a clean, non-formatted document and you can select and apply styles as desired.

~ ~ ~

18. Embedding Graphic Images

Here is the most limiting factor for working with graphics. eInk screens usually display 167 DPI (dots per inch) on their screen at 600 x 800 resolution. This is far less than the average computer display. Here are just a few suggestions.

(1) Keep graphic resolutions in multiples of 167 DPI. This seems to convert clearer. Multiples of 167 seem to work best. 300 DPI images also work well, but working in the eReader native resolution seems to give me a little more clarity and control of my images.

(2) Keep graphics widths to no more than 501 pixels. 501 pixel images are generally not resized.

(3) Anchoring graphics "As Character" seems to keep them in place better.

18.1 How I Embedded My Graphics

(1) I used Wisdom-Soft Screen Hunter 5.1© (download from Internet) to screen capture my images at 96 DPI.

(2) I used Paint.NET© (download from Internet) and copied the captured image from my clipboard to a new image file in Paint.NET.

(3) I resized the image resolution to 167 DPI and the width to 501 pixels.

(4) I saved the images as GIF files.

~ ~ ~

19. Adding Metadata

You will need to add metadata to your eBook before publishing. Metadata (translation: with information) is information about an eDocument such as title, subject, key words, comments, author, etc. Metadata is stored with the eDocument, but is usually not visible within the eDocument itself. In Open Office Writer, metadata is associated with the eDocument's file properties.

Adding metadata to your work is simple. Select **File**, **Properties** form the Main Menu Bar.

The "Properties" pop-up box will be on your screen (see figure 31). Select the **[Description]** tab and enter your information. You may also enter **[Custom Properties]** if desired. Click **[OK]** to save your work.

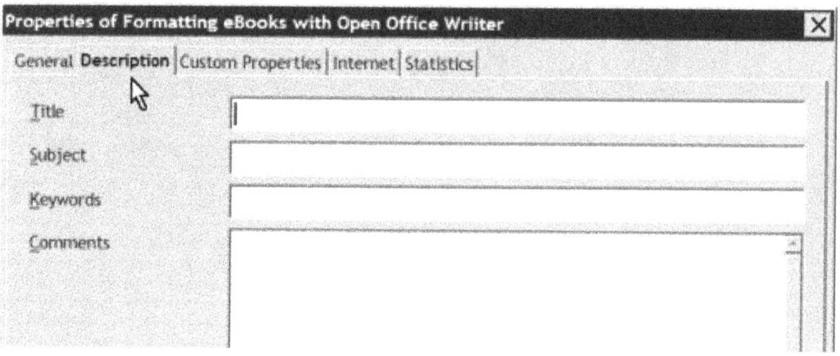

figure 31

~ ~ ~

20. Saving Your Work

Some eConvertors require specific file types for correct processing.

It is always best to work in and save your eDocument in the file format required by your eConvertor.

I have encountered random problems when working in one file format and then "saving as" another format. The "save as" feature may not always keep the specified formatting. For this reason, always work and save in the file format required by your eConvertor.

I do not use RTF for saving my files. I have noticed that with Open Office Writer, RTF will occasionally drop formatting when saved.

~ ~ ~

21. Testing Your Work

Always test your eBooks before distributing them. I cannot stress this enough. Test your eBook before publishing!

You can get a fair idea of what your work will look like by using Open Office Writer's web layout To access the web layout, select **View**, **Web Layout** from the Open Office menu bar. I often re-size my Open Office window to see how my text flows with different size screens.

Mobipocket Creator© and Calibre eBook Management© are both good tools to use to check your work. Both programs are available on the Internet.

The Amazon DTP© (digital text platform) website has some good reference material and guidelines for publishing with Kindle. Of particular interest is the Kindle Generator© and Kindle Previewer©.

Three Press Consulting, Inc.® also has a good open source tool for validating .epub files. It can be accessed at http://threepress.org/document/epub-validate.

You can download various eReader software packages for PC or MAC from the Internet free of charge. They work well. Always download a copy of your published work and verify how it actually displays for readability.

~ ~ ~

22. Connect with Me Online

krbunnsr@gmail.com
http://krbunn.com
http://krbunn.blogspot.com

Document Templates:

You can download my completed eDocument Templates for free. This is my way of saying "thanks."

Template #1 (for eBooks only)can be downloaded free of charge from my website at http://krbunn.com/ebook.html.

Template #2 (for eBooks and 6x9 paperbacks) can be downloaded free of charge from my website at http://krbunn.com/ebook.html.

My Books:

Body Betrayed: My Journey through Sickness and Faith.

Formatting eBooks with Open Office Writer.

Max and Toby (coming soon)

E N D # #